This book is dedicated to my Heavenly Father. Through the Holy Spirit we are empowered to reflect His character because of the shed blood of Jesus Christ, and for this, I thank Him. I pray this book will encourage children of all ages to develop a personal relationship with Him and live a life of forgiveness, freedom, and fullness.

For in Him we live, and move and exist, as even some of your own poets have said, "for we also are His offspring."

—Acts 17:28

Acknowledgments

To those of you who know me, I can only imagine what you are thinking.

Sandy Starnes has authored a children's book! Really?

It goes to show how the Holy Spirit can equip us to do things we consider impossible. "Now to Him who is able to do exceeding abundantly beyond all that we ask or think, according to the power that works within us" (Ephesians 3:20).

To Jesus Christ my Savior, thank you for giving me life beyond measure!

To Holly Payne, thank you for your endless patience with me. Without you, this book would not have reached its potential. You spent countless hours on the phone with me, guiding me through the process. I am always amazed at God's timing. A couple of others were considered to do the illustrations, and yet it was not meant to be. Once I met you, I knew you were the one God would use. The characters came to life as you put pictures to my words. You are the most unselfish person I have ever met. You are my hero!

To my grandchildren, Clairey, TJ, Gabriel, and Elizabeth, thank you for allowing me to use you as characters in the book and for keeping me young at heart. I love you.

To Rhonda Huskins who was the first to proof read "Finley," thank you for your enthusiasm as you assured me it was a really good story. It encouraged me to believe this book might actually get published!

I thank all of you who gave financially to help me publish this book. I can say with absolute confidence that your reward is great in heaven as I believe this book will draw people to know Christ.

To all my family, friends, and my church family, I can't begin to tell you how much I appreciate your love and support of me in so many areas of my life. You have truly been a reflection of God's love for me. Thank you for your sacrificial giving.

Last but not least, thanks to all of you who will read this book. I pray it will be a blessing to you and help you to pass the hope of Christ on to others.

Finley the Fish with Tales From the Sea of Galilee

A Story of Faith

By Sandy Starnes

Illustrated by Holly Payne

Published by Spiritfire Publishing, LLC
www.spiritfirepublishing.com

Spiritfire Publishing is committed to publishing works inspired by the Holy Spirit for the purpose of sharing the Father's love by bringing the message of Jesus Christ and the Gospel of the Kingdom to all nations. The company's foundational Scriptures are Matthew 3:11–12, Mark 16:15–20, Acts 1:8, Acts 2:2–4, and 1 Thessalonians 5:19.

The opinions of the author are not necessarily the same as those of Spiritfire Publishing, LLC.

ISBN: 978-0-9962864-4-2 (Paperback)

ISBN: 978-0-9962864-7-3 (Hardcover)

Previous Edition ISBN: 978-1-63418-423-6 (Paperback)

Finley

"Finley! Ohoooo, Finleeee!" Mama Fin

frantically called out.
Now where could that little fish be?
Mama Fin had been calling her son for several
minutes with no response. It was not like him
to not answer her. Surely, he was all right.
Mama Fin was beginning to get nervous.

This is silly, she thought.

She knew it was not good to worry. Her
parents had taught her to believe in good rather
than evil. Still, there were many dangers lurking
in the waters surrounding their home. It could

be dangerous for a small fish to wander too far away. It was not as if she wanted to be overprotective, but she loved her little fin so much.

She couldn't bear to think of anything bad happening to him!

"My, my, MY!

I must get hold of my thoughts,"

Mama Fin said aloud.

"It is not healthy to let negative thoughts run loose in your head. If you leave them long enough, those thoughts will turn to fear." Mama suddenly felt better after giving herself a pep talk so she decided to call out again, hoping he would respond this time. She said a small prayer for his safe and quick return.

Very loudly, she yelled...

Mama hardly got his name out of her mouth
when she felt a presence come up behind her.
She nearly jumped out of her scales before she
realized it was Finley.

"Hi, Mama."

Finley greeted his mother as he swished up
close to her.

"My goodness, Finley, you scared me!"

Mama exclaimed.
"I'm sorry, Mama. I didn't mean to," he apologized
sincerely.

Where have you been so long?

You didn't get into trouble, did you?

Didn't you hear me call you?"

Mama shot out one question after another, not giving Finley time to answer.

"No, Mama Fin, I didn't get into any trouble. I came as fast as I could when I heard you call me. I was practicing my speed swim," Finley explained.

He knew Mama was not angry. She was just doing what mamas do. Worry. Grand Pappy Fin had told him worry is what mamas do best.

"Mama?"

"Yes, dear."

Her voice seemed more normal now.

"Do you think I have a chance to win the race?"

Finley knew the odds were against him. He was smaller than most of the other fish his age.

"ABSOLUTELY, Finley, you have as much chance as anyone to win. You just keep practicing," Mama assured her young son.

Of course, Finley knew Mama only said that because she was his mother and she knew how badly he wanted to win. Still, it was good to hear her encouraging words.

It was *nice* to have someone believe in him!

Yet he needed more. He needed someone to show him how to have more faith.

Faith means you believe in something you hope for and you believe you will have it even when you cannot see it.

Well, it is *something* like that.

Anyway, he needed to find out more about faith because he definitely hoped to win this race and he could not see how that would ever happen.

"Mama, what do you know about faith?" Finley asked.

She was a little surprised by his question and was not sure how to answer.

"Why don't you go see Grand Pappy Fin? He probably has a story that may help you understand faith and how you can apply it to your problem. You know how much Grand Pappy loves to spend time with you. Besides, he likes nothing better than to tell stories about the people who live above the water. So run along now or it will be too late for you to go today."

Mama nudged him with her nose.

"Thanks, Mama. I won't stay very long," Finley promised as he swam away.

"Just be back before supper," Mama warned.

he called back as he swam toward his
grandfather's home.

Finley was very excited at the thought of
spending time with Grand Pappy Fin.

He knew the best stories and he NEVER
seemed to run out of them. Sometimes, he
would retell the same stories, but no matter
how many times he told them, the ending was
always just as exciting as the first time!

Finley knew his grandfather had been around a

very, **very**, **very**

lonnnnnng time.

Grand Pappy seemed to know a lot about the people who live above the surface of the water. Many of the stories Grand Pappy tells are about those people.

Some of the stories are older than Grand Pappy himself. He heard the stories from his father. Great-Grand Pappy Fin was still living, but he had become too feeble to tell the stories.

He still remembers them, but he keeps **FALLING ASLEEP** while telling them!

Finley felt a little sad that he wasn't old enough to remember when Great-Grand Pappy Fin was younger and could still tell all the stories about the people above the water himself. But at least he had passed the stories on to Grand Pappy!

Without realizing it, Finley had picked up his speed. It would not be long now until he would be at his Grand Pappy's house.

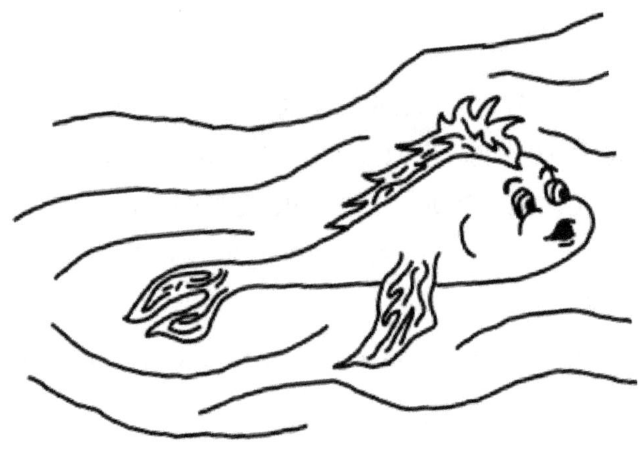

Gang Fish

Finley decided he needed to concentrate on his surroundings.

He was getting near an area that was known for being a hangout for gang fish. These fish were bullies. Papa Fin called them troublemakers. All of a sudden, the water seemed to turn colder and a bit darker.

Finley was not sure, but he thought it might have something to do with the fish that lived in this area. They were mean, and if they caught smaller fish by themselves...

Well, he just did not even want to THINK about what might happen! Maybe Grand Pappy would

have an explanation about the change in the
water or he'd know if Finley just had too much
imagination.

Finley did not like to admit it, but he *WAS* a
little scared of these bullies. Actually...
He was afraid of *MANY* things.
He was secretly afraid of entering this race.
He was not afraid of the race.
It was fear of **FAILURE**.

THERE! He finally admitted it! At least to
himself anyway. But he could not admit it to
anyone else. He did not want his loved ones to
be ashamed of him. Finley shuddered at the
very thought of that.

Wow, the water seems to be getting colder,
Finley thought to himself.

Just about that time, he realized he was not
alone! Out of nowhere, he found several fish
surrounding him and they did NOT look friendly.
One of the larger fish yelled out to one of his
companions, "Hey, Mac, what do you see in the
middle of this circle?"

Mac answered with a sneer.

"Looks like a shrimp to me!"

"Hahahaha!" they all laughed.

The gang began to close in on Finley. The circle became smaller and smaller. Finley realized there was no way out. He tried not to show how afraid he really was.

Maybe they just wanted to tease him and would get tired of their game and let him go. Their next move proved they were not playing. The one called Mac thrust himself at Finley, pushing him violently into another gang fish.

"Hey, what's the big idea?!? Who do you think you are shoving me around like that?" the other fish yelled at Finley.

"I didn't mean to bump into you," Finley apologized. "I need to be on my way."

"Really? Where ya going, shrimp?" Mac mocked.

No doubt about it, he was the leader of the gang.

Finley answered, "To my grandfather's house."

With great disgust in his voice, Mac replied, "Listen to the baby shrimp. He's going to his grandfather's house. Is he a shrimp like you?"

All the members of the gang laughed, except for one of them. He kept quiet and stayed at a slight distance from the circle. Finley had been watching him out of the corner of his eye. He wondered why the fish was there, because he did not seem to want to participate with his friends in terrorizing Finley.

The remark about his grandfather made Finley angry.

"He's no shrimp! He is powerful, and you better hope he doesn't find you bothering me, because he will make you sorry!"

"Oh yeah? I'll make you sorry you swam into

my territory, you puny little shrimp!"
Mac roared.

He began to charge toward Finley.

NOW Finley was in *serious* trouble. He knew he was no match for this fish even if he had not been scared.

Finley remembered what his Grand Pappy always told him. He could almost hear him say,

"Son, if you ever find yourself in trouble and you see no way out, call upon the Lord of the Heaven and the Earth and the Seas and he will help you."

Finley began to pray silently for the Lord to send him some help.

All of a sudden, the fish that stayed back
during the attack swam over, quickly putting
himself between Finley and Mac!

He spoke in a calm but strong voice.

*"Come on, we are wasting our time, let's
go and do something else."*

"What's the matter with you? Are you

getting cold fins or something? You're not

going soft on me are you?"
Mac sneered even more.

"No, of course not. I just don't want to spend all my time today picking on someone smaller than me," the challenger replied.

"Well, well, well," Mac exclaimed, "I think we have a mutiny on our hands, fellers."

Finley thought it might have been better if the fish had not spoken up. It seemed to make their leader ANGRIER than ever.

He seemed to forget about Finley for the moment and focused his attention on the fish challenging his leadership.

When Finley saw the attention was no longer on him, he thought it might be a perfect time to slip away.

As Finley began to inch toward the opening of
the circle, he had a change of heart.

Suddenly, he knew he could not just abandon
the fish who tried to help him. Not knowing
what else to do, he watched as the argument
grew.

The challenger held his
position.
    He did NOT EVEN
            FLINCH!

The leader spoke in a very loud voice, "I'll give

you to the count of three to swim away.

            One... Two... THREE!"

The challenger STILL did not move a muscle.

The leader became furious.

"I told you to MOVE!"

Very clearly and firmly, the challenger said, "*No,
I will not.*"

There was complete silence. The water became
deathly still as the two fish stood their ground.

Now they faced each other as if they had
forgotten they had ever been friends.

The look on each of their faces made it clear
they were no longer friendly.

The leader was summing up the situation.

Before he could make a move, the other fish in
the gang began to speak up.

One of them said, "LET IT GO. There are
other things more important to do."

The leader realized the challenger was not going
to budge and his other friends were actually
giving him a way out. He took it. He and the
other fish began to swim away.

The leader left with a threat hanging in the air.

"Don't even THINK this is the last you're

gonna hear from me, you traitor! You and the

shrimp better always look over your shoulder

because you never know where I might show

up."

Finley saw that the challenger did not swim off
with the others.

For a moment, he did not know what to say.

Finally, he spoke.
"You probably just made some enemies.
Aren't you worried?"

"*Nah,*" the challenger answered. "I was getting tired of their tricks and was looking for a good reason to separate myself from them. There has to be better things to do than cause trouble all the time. Besides, I am not worried about them. *They are mostly just talk.*"

"Well," replied Finley, "it sure is good for me you decided to make your stand today. *You probably saved me from getting my fins broken.* Thank you."

"You are welcome. Actually, I decided that today was the day to change because of something *YOU* did."

"Really?" Finley asked in surprise. "What did I do?"

"Well, I couldn't be sure, but I thought you were praying."

"I was, but HOW did you know? I didn't say anything out loud, did I?"

Finley felt a little embarrassed at the thought of being heard.

After a brief moment, the challenger answered, "You didn't say anything out loud, but you had the same look on your face that my mom has when she prays. *It made me think about my life and where it is going, and to be honest with you, I did not like who I was becoming*. I have never prayed before. It must be a good thing, so maybe I'll give it a try sometimes."

Finley, still amazed at the way things had worked out, replied, "You sure were an answer to my prayer today."

"*WOW! Are you KIDDING me?*" The challenger let out a stream of bubbles in his excitement. "*I don't think I have ever been an answer to prayer before!*"

Finley suddenly remembered he did not even know his new friend's name.

"What's your name?" Finley asked.

"*Arnie.*"

"Arnie?!? What kind of name is THAT?"

Finley felt like sticking his fin in his big mouth the moment he said it.

"I'm sorry, that was very unkind of me. I just never heard of a fish named Arnie before."
"*It's okay, I get that a lot,*" Arnie said.

"Hey, I've got a great idea! We can call you...

CHALLENGER!

After all, you **did** challenge the leader. What do you think about that name?"

Finley desperately wanted to find a way to keep Arnie as a friend.

"*I like it, yeah, I like it a lot!* Challenger it is," Arnie agreed. "You haven't told me your name yet."

"Finley. My name is Finley and I think we are going to be good friends. That is if you don't mind having a 'SHRIMP' for a friend."

Finley laughed.

Challenger laughed too and said, "If you don't mind a friend named Arnie, I guess I can handle a 'shrimp' for a friend."

"So, Finley, are you *really* going to see your grandfather?"

"Yes, would you like to come with me?" Finley asked, hoping his new friend would say yes.

"Sure, why not? Will he mind if you bring me along?"

"Nah, he loves visitors. Besides, he will be glad to know I have made a new friend. It will be great to tell him a good story and the way you and I met is definitely a good story," Finley answered.

Challenger moved his head in agreement. "It sure is a good story. So what do you do at your grandfather's house?"

"Mostly listen to stories, although some of them happened a long time ago."

"Stories about *what*?" Challenger asked.

"All sorts of stories! A lot of them are about the people that live above the water. It seems the people are connected to the Lord of the Heavens and the Earth and the Seas.

HE is the One I prayed to today.

Grand Pappy says that the Lord cares about all His creatures above the water and all of us below too," Finley explained.

"You think He, the Lord I mean, *really exists?* Maybe your grandfather makes up those stories?"

This troubled Finley, but he did not want to offend his new friend, so he just said, "Come with me and you can decide for yourself if the stories are true or not. Anyway, it is very interesting to hear about the people above the water."

"Have you EVER seen any of them?"

Challenger was asking out of curiosity because he had never seen any humans before but had heard about them.

"Yes! Once, I was very near the top of the water and I could hear them talking. I saw one of them when He leaned over and He looked STRAIGHT at me.

It was the strangest thing I ever experienced!

It was as if I had known him all my life and yet I had never seen him before.

I know that sounds crazy, but if that is not weird enough for you, what I will tell you NEXT is even CRAZIER!

When he looked into my eyes, I have never felt such PEACE before."

Finley shivered just thinking about it. "I never told anyone about that, not even my Grand Pappy. I am not sure why I told you, so maybe it could be our secret."

Challenger had a **strange** feeling as he listened to Finley's story.

It must have shown because Finley asked about it.

"My goodness, Challenger! You have the *strangest* look on your face! What is the MATTER with you?"

"Well, because that is *EXACTLY* how I felt today when I stood against the leader of the gang. I knew somehow I wasn't supposed to do *anything* wrong to you, and when I made up my mind to do the RIGHT thing, I didn't have ANY fear, just peace. The only time I ever felt anything like that was once when my mother prayed for me. She was worried that I was running with the wrong crowd.

Although I didn't understand about prayer, I felt this *incredible* sense of peace as she prayed.

"I'm telling you, Finley, it was *STRANGE*. So if you will keep my secret, I will keep yours. I mean, can you just *imagine* what those characters I used to run with would do with a story *like THAT?*"

"It is too scary to think about," Finley shuddered.

The two friends swam toward Grand Pappy's home. One of the great benefits of having a

friend to share the journey with is that it
doesn't seem to take as long to get there.
Challenger broke the silence.

"What are you going to see your
        grandfather about today?
    Are you just going to hear another
                        story?
It's not that I would MIND hearing his
stories.
        I just wondered what to expect."

Finley answered him by asking a question,

    "Have you ever heard of faith?"

"Nope, can't say that I have. What is it
and what is it for?"

"Well," said Finley, "that is what I am going to
ask my Grand Pappy about. But it has
SOMETHING to do with believing in something
you can't see, but you know that it is real."

"You sure are *one strange little fish*, Finley, but I *will* say this for you. There is something different about you. I mean that in a good kind of way, of course."

Finley felt a little embarrassed so he changed the subject.

"Hey look! We are almost there. Just around this seaweed.

Oh, I guess I should warn you! Sometimes Grand Pappy is a little hard of hearing so you have to talk a little louder than normal."

"I hope he likes me! Since I live on your way here, maybe you would let me come with you again."

Challenger didn't want to be too pushy, but he didn't have any grandparents.

"I'm SURE he will like you, and I would appreciate your company anytime," Finley assured his new friend.

Grand Pappy Fin

The two fish finally arrived at Grand Pappy's home. The many different colors of seaweed and shells lining the path to his doorway were bright and cheerful. Challenger was very excited.

He somehow KNEW this was going to be a very important meeting for him. Just about that time, he heard Finley yell.

"Hello, Grand Pappy! I brought my new friend to meet you!"

Challenger was *amazed* at the size of Finley's grandfather.

He was very large, and although you could tell he was old, he still appeared to be VERY strong.

"Finley, my boy! Come on in and bring your friend. It is so good to see you."

Grand Pappy's voice matched his size. It was loud, yet gentle, all at the same time.

"Grand Pappy, I want you to meet my new friend. His name is Arnie, but I call him Challenger."

"Well, Challenger, it is good to meet you. I don't know how you came up with Challenger out of Arnie, but any friend of my grand fin is a friend of mine. *Welcome to my home."*

"Thank you, sir. It is good to meet you."

Challenger instantly liked Grand Pappy Fin.

However, he didn't know what to call him. Grand Pappy must have read his mind.

"You may call me G.P., that is short for Grand Pappy. Would you prefer I call you Arnie or Challenger?"

"You may call me Arnie. Challenger is what Finley calls me because of the way we met."

G.P. let out a peal of laughter, sending a burst of bubbles into every direction.

"I can't wait to hear your story, so come on in and get comfortable. Now, tell me of this great adventure and then I will tell you a story about something I saw yesterday."

Finley began to tell the story and became so excited, his words came tumbling out too fast.

Challenger took over telling the story and Finley would calm down and take back over again.

FINALLY, after switching back and forth, they told the whole adventure.

G.P.'s head was going back and forth as the two young fish told their tale.

"Oh my goodness!" G.P. exclaimed.

"That was QUITE an adventure you two had. Seems to me, Arnie, you were an answer to a prayer, and I thank you for doing the right thing. It sounds as if my grand fin would have been hurt if you had not stopped those renegade fish.

I am glad that you are not running with those troublemakers any longer. I will get some of the grown-ups to patrol those waters for a while to make sure those gang fish will not have the opportunity to cause any more trouble."

Challenger was the first to speak up.

"Finley tells me you like to tell stories about the people who live above the water.
Do you *REALLY* get stories from what you see and hear or do you just make them up?"

G.P. let out a roar of laughter.

"I like the way you get right to the point, Arnie.

39

I have been in these waters a long, **looong** time and have seen many things going on. My Pappy used to tell me stories about the folk who live above the water. Pappy would tell me stories about things that happened in waters far away too. Some of the stories were even handed down from his Pappy and Grand Pappy."

"*Like what kind of stories?*" Challenger could hardly sit still as he asked questions.

"Oh well, let me see. For example, one of the stories that was passed down by my Great-Grand Pappy. You know the waters we live in are big. Yes sir, *very big*, but there is a great body of water called the Red Sea and it is a lot bigger than where we live. Why, the story is that once a man was told by the Lord of the Heavens, the Earth, and the Seas to hold out his staff over the water and then the water parted and many people walked across on dry land!"

G. P. stopped to take his breath, and before he could start again, Challenger blurted out.
"What is a staff?"

Finley spoke up because he had heard part of the story before and had asked the same question.

"It's a long stick that people use for many things."

Challenger's thoughts were racing.

"If this sea is so far away, how did your Great-Grand Pappy find out? It's not connected to our water, is it?"

G.P. could tell this young fish had a lot of brainpower.

"That's a great question, my friend. We get news from other sources. Sometimes, the seagulls talk to us when they land on drifting wood from sunken ships. Then there are always the turtles. Now they are some *real talkers*, and because they live part time on the land, they see a lot and come out here to tell us what's going on."

Before Challenger could ask another question,

G.P. assured them he would tell the story of the Red Sea another time. He wanted to find out Finley's reason for visiting today. He knew his grand fin had something on his mind.

"Finley, you must have something important on your mind, so go ahead and spit it out."

Grand Pappy urged his grand fin to speak up. Finley fumbled around, looking for the right words. He could not seem to find a smart way to ask, so he just took a deep breath and hoped he wouldn't sound too dumb.

"I need to know more about faith, and Mama said I should ask you to explain it to me."

G.P. smiled in his understanding way and said, "Now what was so hard about that?

Let's see.

Faith is a bit difficult to explain because it is something you cannot see.

I think I have a story that might make it easier to understand.

Get comfortable, boys, and I will tell you something I witnessed just yesterday."

Grand Pappy Fin settled into his favorite patch of seaweed and let out a stream of bubbles. That usually meant what he had seen earlier must be very interesting. Finley could hardly wait for him to start!

Grand Pappy always paused before beginning his story. It was his time of prayer. However, this time he did something different.

Instead of praying silently, he prayed aloud.

"Father of all the Heavens, and the Earth, and the Seas I ask your wisdom and help as I proclaim your goodness to these young fish. Help me to show them your power. Amen."

Challenger had a strange and confused look on his face as G.P. finished praying so Grand Pappy asked him. "What's troubling you, Arnie?"

"How do you know He hears you or that He even cares?"

Challenger desperately wanted to believe, but it seemed strange to talk to someone you cannot see.

"FAITH, my boy!

And that is what I am going to try and explain so you can understand. The Lord created *everything* and He created everything for *His*

purpose. He has a purpose for your existence.
It was His plan to let us live in this sea and
He expects us to take care of His creation,"
G.P. explained with excitement.

Challenger remarked, "*I still don't get it, but
I will listen and try to understand.*"

"Very well," G.P. replied. "Let's get on
with the story."

The storm

Grand Pappy Fin was sure he had the young fishes' attention as he began.

"I could feel a storm brewing on the surface of the water. The winds pick up **very** quickly on this lake, and before you know it, anyone in or on this lake could find themselves in a LOT of trouble. The storms that rise up can tear a small boat to pieces! It can also be dangerous for fish caught unaware. Being that I am on the Watch-Out Brigade—"

Challenger interrupted, *"What is a Watch-Out Brigade?"*

Although Grand Pappy Fin did not like to be interrupted while telling a story, he was very patient with Finley's new friend.

"We are a group of older, more experienced fish that look out for problems caused by sudden storms. At the first sign of trouble, we go to the surface to make sure everyone is safe."

"*Sorry,*" Challenger apologized. "*I'll try not to interrupt you again.*"

"That's okay, but let's get on with the story or we won't have time to finish it before you need to leave. I do not want your parents to worry. As I was saying, it was my turn to patrol the waters yesterday, and everything seemed normal UNTIL the evening came. It was very late when I sensed the winds picking up and felt the water become very choppy. I quickly went to the surface, and *sure enough*, there was a storm building. It did not take long for the winds to cause great waves to crash into each other. I checked to see that all the fish had taken cover deep into the water for safety. I was about to take a dive myself when I saw a boat filled with men.

It was very noisy with the
winds HOWLING and the waves CRASHING!

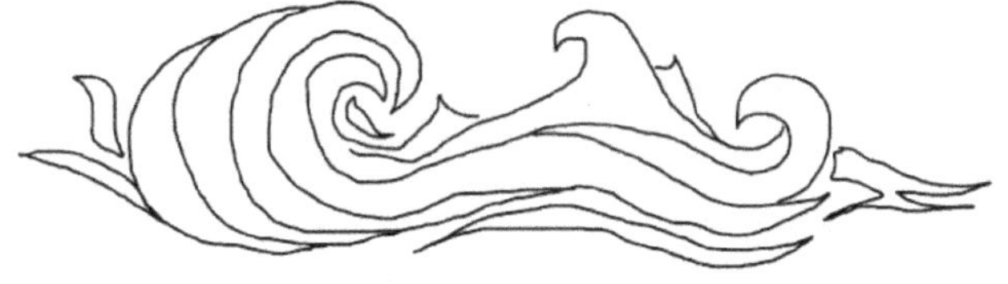

It was very frightening for me and I live here.
Although the noise of the storm was very
LOUD, I could hear the men calling out in fear.

"Then a VERY strange thing happened. A man
came walking on top of the water! I have seen
many strange things and heard even stranger
stories in my time but NEVER have I EVER
witnessed a man walking on the water! The
waves and wind did not seem to bother Him. It
looked as if he was going to walk right by the
boat. The man seemed unaware that a storm
was going on.

*He just walked on the water as if he
belonged there!*

The men in the boat saw the one on the water
and began to cry out, 'IT'S A GHOST!'"

49

Before G.P. could go on with the story,
Challenger asked...

"What is a ghost?"

Grand Pappy did not mind not knowing
everything, but he did not want to appear to be
ignorant so he tried to avoid the question.

"That is not really important, but I will tell you
this. Whatever a ghost is, those men
SURE were frightened of it."

Finley wished his friend would stop interrupting
because he was interested to see what this

story had to do with faith and how that could help him win the race.

He urged his Grand Pappy on. "Go on, Grand Pappy, tell us what happened next."

"Well, when the man walking on the water heard that they thought he was a ghost, he called out and said...

'Take courage. Don't be afraid, it is I.'

"One of the men in the boat said to him, 'Lord, if it is you, command me to come to you on the water.'"

Grand Pappy paused, and in a very low voice, he said, "That is when I realized I was about to witness a MIRACLE.

The one walking on the water is the Son of God.
He is the one they call Jesus.

I have heard tales of this Jesus from some of
the seagulls, and occasionally, I hear bits of
conversation from people on the boats about
Him."

The two young fish were
glued to their seats. They
had never heard a story
like this one before.
Finley was the first to
speak. "Did the man get
out of the boat?"

"Yes," Grand Pappy
answered. "Jesus held
out his hand and said,

'Come.'

The man—they called him Peter—got out of the
boat and walked toward Jesus. He just kept
looking at the face of Jesus. Then suddenly,
this Peter began to sink into the water and he
cried out to Jesus. 'Lord, save me!'
"Jesus then asked,

'Why do you have such little faith?

Why do you doubt?'

"At that time, I thought for SURE the man
Peter was going to drown. But Jesus took
Peter by the hand and they walked back to the
boat together and *just like that,*" Grand
Pappy flipped his fins to demonstrate how fast
the next event happened. "The very second
they stepped into the boat, the wind stopped
blowing and the waves calmed down. Then all
the men in the boat began to worship Jesus
and say,

'You ARE the Son of God!'"

The young fish had many questions. However, as
usual, Challenger gushed out with a question
that had not crossed Finley's mind.

G.P. said, "Arnie, you sure know how to ask difficult questions.

Worship is showing love and devotion to the one who is superior over you.

The only one who is superior is the Creator. Just in case you are wondering, I will remind you our Creator is the God of all the Heavens and the Earth and the Seas."

Finley was in deep thought, trying to figure out exactly what he needed to ask. Of course, he wanted to know what faith meant, and since the man, Jesus, told Peter he had little faith, Finley figured that was a good place to start.

"Grand Pappy, why did Peter sink? It was easy to see he could walk on the water and why did Jesus say to him that Peter had little faith? Why did the winds and the waves calm down when they got back into the boat?"

"WHOA, hold on, boy, one question at a time!
I will start by answering your last question.
The winds and the waves calmed down
because the One who created them has
power over them and all things were
created by Him and have to obey His will."

Once again, Challenger interrupted with another
question.

"Well, if it was
His will for the
man named Peter
to walk on water,
WHY did he sink?"

Grand Pappy could see Challenger was one of
those fish who did not take everything at face
value.

He wanted to know the WHY of everything.
Challenger was a deep thinker.

G.P. tried to explain.

"People have the right to choose what they do. The Creator wants them to obey Him because He knows that things will be better for them if they do, but still, it IS their choice.

"Faith is about trust. When Peter got out of the boat, he trusted Jesus more than what was going on around him.

However, when Peter began to take his eyes off Jesus and look at the winds and the waves, he began to sink. Jesus told him he had little faith because Peter thought the winds and the waves were stronger than the One who created them. As long as Peter trusted Jesus more than his circumstances, he could STAY on top of the water. Faith is about believing and trusting the Lord, no matter what is going on around you."

Challenger asked G.P, *"How did you learn all this stuff?"*

Grand Pappy laughed.

"I learned by asking questions and listening to those with more experience in life than I have. *You will do well, Arnie, if you ask the right questions and then use the answers to bring good into your life.* Here is some advice for both of you.

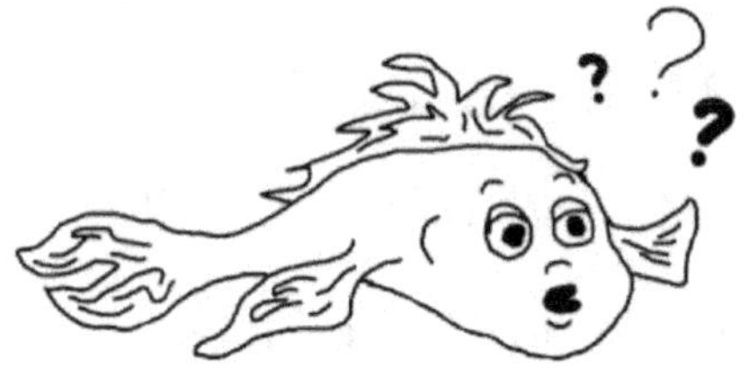

*Never be afraid to
ask the Lord for help."*

Finley spoke up and asked, "How do we know He will answer us?"

Grand Pappy answered with a question.

"Finley, what happened when you were surrounded by those gang fish and you prayed?"

"Challenger came to my rescue."

Grand Pappy wanted to make a point.

"That was not a coincidence, Finley. You asked for help and help was given. The Lord showed you He heard you and cared enough about you to answer. Finley, it took FAITH to ask and the Lord is trying to build your faith by giving you what you ask for."

Challenger asked, *"Does that mean He will give you anything you ask for?"*

"No, Arnie, He knows what is best for you and what will help you serve His purpose, so what you ask for has to be His will. He will not give you something that will harm you and He will not go against your will. If you want something and choose to do it even though you know it is wrong, He will not stop you. And Arnie, did you realize that the Lord did not just answer

Finley's prayer for help? *He helped you as well."*

Puzzled by G.P.'s words, Arnie asked, *"How did He help me?"*

"You said your mother prayed for you and you had been looking for a way to break free from the gang you were hanging out with. The Lord knows what is in our hearts and He used the opportunity to give you a way out and to help Finley at the same time.

That is the goodness of our Creator." G.P. spoke in a very quiet voice.

"Wow!" Challenger let out a stream of bubbles as if he had been holding his breath.

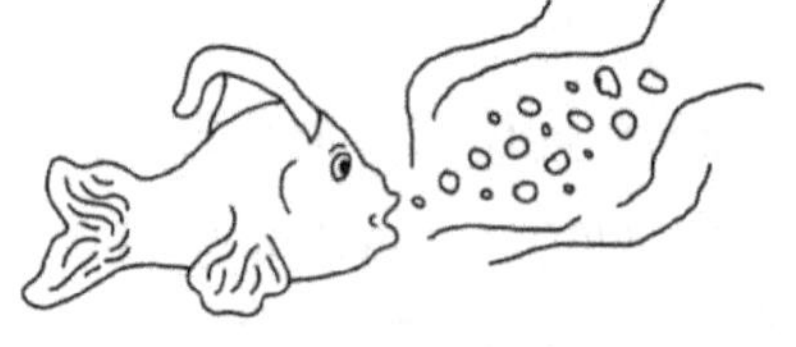

"All this stuff is going to take some time to understand. But it was an awesome story. Maybe sometime, you will take me and Finley to the surface to listen to the people in the boats."

"Sure I will." G.P. assured him. "I'll keep my ears open, and if I hear of something going on, I'll give you both a call."

Finley wanted to make sure Grand Pappy remembered the race.

"Grand Pappy, will you come to see me in the race Saturday? Please??"

"I wouldn't miss it for the world, don't you worry.

You are going to do all right. Besides, it will be a LOT of fun. Don't be so concerned about winning that you miss the best part," Grand Pappy said with a slight grin.

Finley seemed confused at Grand Pappy's words. "You mean it is wrong to want to win? What could be better than winning the race?"

"No, no, no, of course not, after all, it is a race. Someone is going to take home a prize, and it might as well be you. *Just don't forget to have fun along the way and learn something through the experience. Then if you should not be the winner, you STILL will take something home with you.*

Finley, don't worry about your size. Being smaller than the other fish in the race does not have to put you at a disadvantage. Remember Peter. He was not made to walk on water, but the Lord can help you do what seems to be impossible.

Practice, keep a right attitude, and trust the Lord with all your heart and you will always be a winner."

Grand Pappy wanted his grand fin to understand that **winning is NOT always the most important thing.**

"You boys better be on your way.
I wouldn't want your mamas to worry about you.
I will see you at the race on Saturday, Finley.
Will you be going to the race, Arnie?

"I don't know. I haven't thought about it,"
Challenger shrugged his fins as he answered.

Finley spoke up quickly.

"Please come, Challenger, it would be easier for me if I knew I had someone besides my family pulling for me."

"Sure, in that case, I would like to be there to see you race."

Challenger had hoped he would be invited.

"*Come along, boys.* I'll see you across the way past the area where those gang fish hang out," Grand Pappy Fin assured them.

"You'll be safe enough. Don't play around and be late for supper."

The three fish made their way past the colorful seashells that lined the path into Grand Pappy's home.

Challenger spoke up first, "*Your home sure is very nice, G.P., especially the path lined with the beautiful shells. Did you do all that work by yourself?*"

Grand Pappy did not answer. Challenger looked over to see why and he saw a look of sadness on G.P.'s face.

"I'm sorry, G.P., if I asked something that is none of my business."

"Not at all, Arnie." G.P. answered. "It's just that your question took me back to a very happy time of my life. Finley's Grandmother Fin did all the pretty work on the path. She loved to work in her sea yard. It always makes me a little sad when I think of those days because I miss her so much. She was a very special ladyfish. She is the one who taught me how to pray and trust the Lord of all creation."

The three fish finally made it past the danger zone, so they quickly said their good-byes. The two young fins moved at a steady speed toward home. As Grand Pappy Fin turned back toward his home, he waved his fin and was soon out of sight.

As usual, Challenger had more questions.

"What happened to your Grandmother Fin?"

"I don't know a LOT about it. My family thinks I am too young to understand. It had something to do with the people on the water and their fishing nets."

"What is a fishing net?"

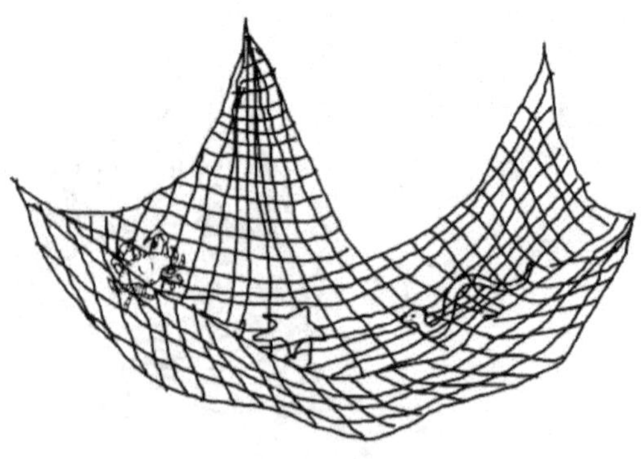

"My goodness, Challenger, don't you know ANYTHING?"

Challenger might have been offended at his new friend's attitude if he had not understood why Finley sounded so irritated.

Challenger had already learned that when Finley did not answer a question, it was because he really did not know the answer. Breaking into a fit of laughter, he pointed at Finley and said, *"You don't know what a fishing net is, do you?"*

Finley might have been embarrassed with someone else, but Challenger seemed to know how to say something without humiliating him. So he felt comfortable in admitting to Challenger that he was not sure about the fishing net.

"Not really, so I guess that makes two of us who don't know everything," Finley laughed too.

"I guess you are right about that," Challenger continued to giggle.

"Well, Finley, this is where I turn off to get to my home. Maybe you will come by one day and meet my family."

"Sure, Challenger, I would like that and you can meet my parents when you come to the race on Saturday."

Finley was only a short way from home and he could not WAIT to tell his family about his great adventures.

Home was now in sight, and Finley realized how very tired he was. He could not ever remember having such a WONDERFUL and EXCITING day. It had been a real adventure!

Finley was almost to the door of his home
when he saw his Papa inspecting the seaweed
that grew on the side of the house.

"Hi, Papa, what are you doing?"
Finley asked his father.

"Well, son, I was just looking around while
waiting to see if you were near. Your mother was
getting a little concerned because you were not
home yet. I am glad to see you safely home and
now your mother can rest. How was your Grand
Pappy today?"

"I hope Mama
wasn't too
worried, because...

I had a terrific day!

Grand Pappy is fine and sends his love to the family. He will be at the race on Saturday."

Finley hoped Mama was not in a bad mood.

He wanted to share ALL his adventures with his family.

"Come on in, Finley, Mama has supper ready and you may tell us why your day was so TERRIFIC!"
Papa said with a laugh.

During supper, Finley told his family all about how he met Challenger and the way he helped Finley escape the gang fish.

"My goodness, Finley, WHAT A DAY!"

Mama Fin exclaimed.

"But did you learn anything about faith?

"Oh, sure, I did. You know Grand Pappy has a story about **everything** and he told Challenger and me about a man who...

WALKED...
ON...
THE...
WATER!

I think I understand a little more about faith now," Finley explained.

Mama wasn't sure how all this tied in to winning the race, but it was getting late, and she wanted her little fin to get ready for bed.

"Well, Finley, I am sure you have more

to tell, but you look very tired and I

want you to get some sleep. Say your

prayers and sleep well, son."

Mama gave him a kiss and sent him on his way.

"Good night, Mama. Good night, Papa."

The Big Day

Finley woke very early without anyone's help. It took him a few minutes to collect his thoughts and figure out why he felt such excitement.

SUDDENLY, it hit him!

He had been waiting for this day!

Now that it was here, Finley felt very nervous. Of course, he began giving himself a pep talk.

After all, it WAS what he had been training for. He remembered all the practice and how could he forget?

HE HAD FAITH!

He also had the support of all his family. And his new friend, Challenger, would be there to cheer for him too. Finley still felt a little nervous and then he remembered how prayer always seemed to bring him peace. If he was going to let faith help, he decided he needed to practice using faith.

He began to pray out loud...

"Dear Lord of the Heavens and Earth and the Seas, I ask you to help me today to swim with great speed. I will trust you today to help me be the best I can be. I would like my family and friends to be proud of me. Help me not to worry about the others around me that are larger and faster than I am. Please help me to have more faith. Thank You."

Finley was not sure how you were supposed to end a prayer, but he figured the Lord would understand that Finley meant well.

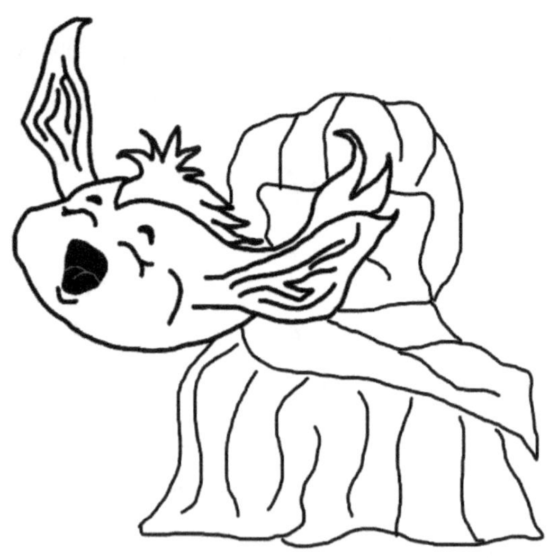

Finley leaped from his bed of seaweed, stretching his fins as he went to find some breakfast. Mama was putting breakfast on the table made from seashells.

"Good morning, Finley! Are you ready for the race?" Mother Fin asked her son.

"Yes, Mama. I prayed this morning about the race. I hope the Creator heard me."

"Don't be silly, Finley. Of course, He heard you and He will not forget you. He is always there for us. He will be with you all the way," Mama Fin assured her son.

Mama sounded surer than Finley felt, but it did not matter how he felt. He was determined to have faith and not let doubts take over his thoughts. Besides, in two more hours, the race would begin and he had to be ready.

"Thanks for breakfast, Mama!" Finley shouted as he raced out the door.

"Sorry, Papa! I have a little time before the race and I want to practice some."

"Well, it probably wouldn't be a bad idea to stretch your fins a little, but you don't want to use up all your energy," Papa Fin warned. "Hey, I have a great idea, why don't you swim as fast as you can and I'll time you. When I say 'Go,' you swim as quickly as possible to that cove over there and back."

Papa pointed out the target area as he gave instructions.

Finley was very excited that Papa wanted to help him. He knew his father loved him, but he was always so busy and he hardly had time to spend with Finley. This was going to make the day more special than expected.

Finley took his place at the starting place as his father called out.

Like a SHOT, Finley sailed toward his goal!

Before he knew it, he was at the mouth of the cove. He turned with ease and headed back toward his father. It was only a short distance, but still...it gave Finley a feeling of confidence!

"VERY GOOD, Finley! Not only did you swim very fast, but you *glided* through the water too. You just do that during the race and you will be bringing home a trophy!"

Papa Fin spoke with great pride to his son. Seeing his dad look at him with pride caused Finley to think that it was almost as good as winning the race. ALMOST!

"Should I do it again, Papa? Just to warm up?" Finley asked.

"No, I think that is enough for now. Maybe you should relax with a good book. You will get warmed up on the way to the race."

"Thanks, Papa," Finley said warmly.

"You are welcome, son. Don't you worry now, you are going to do just FINE!" Papa Fin assured his son.

Finley swam off toward his room with the feeling anything was possible, even winning the race. It was a great feeling.

Finley decided that reading was not the thing he needed to do the most. Actually, he felt like praying.

This was very new to him and it caused him to wonder why he felt the need to pray.

At that very moment, a terrible thought hit him.

Was he just using prayer as a way to get the Lord to help him win the race?

That would be TERRIBLE to use His goodness like that. These thoughts troubled the young fish. Suddenly, Finley turned and swam quickly to the place he knew his father would be.

Finley approached his father, calling out, "Papa!"

Seeing the look on Finley's face startled his father.

"What is wrong, son, you look terrified. Has something happened to your mother?"

"No, Papa. I have some terrible thoughts and I don't know what to do about them," Finley cried.

"Calm down, son. I am sure it cannot be that bad. Tell me what you are thinking that is so terrible and we will deal with it," Papa Fin said in a soothing voice.

Finley began to tell his father how he felt like praying, but he was afraid it was just to win the race.

Finley's father had a very serious look on his face and, in a voice to match his expression, he said, "The Lord of all creation knows what is in your heart, but if you feel like you are doing something for the wrong reason, that could be His way of showing you how to let Him change your wrong thinking into right thinking. He is VERY understanding, so just repent."

"Repent?" Finley was very confused. "What does that mean?"

"Repent means to ask forgiveness for a wrong that has been done and then change the way you think so that you can do what is right. Just ask Him to forgive you for wrong thoughts and ask Him to show you the right way to think about this race. You can trust Him because He loves to help His creatures when they are serious about doing right."

Finley was amazed at his father's wisdom.

"Thanks, Papa. I did not know you knew so much about the Lord. I feel better and I am ready to repent. Will you stay with me while I pray?"

"Of course I will, son. I will also pray after you have taken care of business with the Lord," Papa declared.

Finley closed his eyes and lifted his head upward.

"Dear Lord, I am sorry for being selfish. I did not mean to use prayer just to get my way. Please forgive me and help me to have the right attitude about this race. I really want to win, but I think I want to please you more than I want to win. Win or lose, I hope I will be the fish you could be proud of. Lord, thank you for my Papa. He is a great father. Amen."

Papa Fin was good to his word as he prayed, "Lord, you are so good to us. You have given us a home and a wonderful family. Help me to be a father to this  young fish that would reflect your goodness. I ask you to keep Finley safe while he competes in this race. Help him to be a good sport and a good teammate. Amen."

Papa Fin stroked Finley with his fin and said, "I am very proud of you, son. You will do well in this life. Now you had better get ready. It is time to leave! You do not want to be late. I will get your mother."

Finley left his father with a new sense of contentment. He still intended to swim to win. After all that was the whole point of entering the race.

Winning just did not seem to be the MOST important thing anymore. Finley did not understand exactly why, but maybe he could figure it out in time.

Finley could see the family waiting outside the door of their home. He swam up just as his mother was about to call out to him.

"Oh, there you are, Finley. It is time to go.

Are you ready for your big day?" Mama Fin asked.

"I guess so. I suppose I am a little scared," Finley admitted to his family.

"You will do fine," Mama Fin replied.

Finley could hear someone calling his name. By the sound of it, the voice was calling from the surface of the water.

"Hey! That sounds like Gabe the Seagull. May I go to the surface to see what he wants? Please? It will only take a few minutes and I will join up with you before you get to the race pool," Finley pleaded.

"Sure, Finley, but don't stay too long," Papa responded to his son's request.

Finley could see Gabe the Seagull as he reached the top. Gabe was perched on some driftwood.

The rest of his Land Crew friends gathered around.

Finley stuck his head just above the surface as he greeted them.

"Hi, Gabe. What's going on?"

"Finley, it is so good to see you, my boy!"
Gabe shouted.

Gabe tended to speak too loudly. Maybe it had
something to do with the wind blowing in his
ears above the water.

Gabe also dragged his words out so much that
it made Finley want to laugh. He did not want
to hurt his friend's feelings, so he kept his
laughter to himself.

"Well," Gabe began slowly. "I just wanted
to wish you well in the race. TJ.

the Turtle and Lizzy the Lizard
and Clairey the Sand Crab and I
will be waiting on the shore for the
outcome and we will be praying for
you to win."

"Gee, thanks, Gabe, that is one of the
nicest things I have ever heard. It sure is
great to have friends like you and the rest
of the Land Crew. I will send you word
as soon as possible. I have to get going or
I'll be late."

They all waved goodbye as Finley turned to
swim away with a smile on his face.

"Maybe T.J. the Turtle will take a
dive to see what is happening
before the race is over!" Gabe yelled as
Finley swam away.

The Race

Finley found his parents in the place they had agreed to meet.

After getting his racing number, he had just enough time to make sure he knew the spot from where his parents would be watching.

He was very excited to see Grand Pappy Fin there. Looking around, he spotted Challenger. He quickly called out for him to come over.

He introduced Challenger to his parents.

Challenger was very glad to see G. P. again.

"It is time for me to go," Finley said nervously.

Challenger spoke up,
"Go get 'em, Finley!
You can do it!"

With that word of confidence, Finley swam
toward the starting line.

There were about ten fish in the lineup. Just
as Finley thought, he WAS the smallest fish. One
other fish was not *much* bigger than Finley, but
still bigger IS bigger.

Finley remembered his prayer, and at that
moment, he made up his mind, win or lose, he
was going to do his best and trust the Lord.

The official of the race called all contestants
to order. He went over the rules and then
announced that it was time to begin.

Finley took a deep breath and slowly let out a
stream of bubbles.

Just before the official started the count, Finley caught a glimpse of a familiar fish to his right.

He turned his head to get a better view, and to his horror...

HE SAW MAC!

Mac was the one who had attacked him on the way to his Grand Pappy's house.

Almost in a whisper, Mac spoke,

"Well, look who is beside me, it's the shrimp.

You'd better watch your back, shrimp, not

that I plan to be behind you, but I think

you get my point."

This really was an unexpected twist. Finley never dreamed he would have to race against his worst enemy. He almost froze with fear, but the official was already calling out the start.

Like a shot, all the fish pushed forward. Each fish was trying to get ahead of the others.

Surprisingly, it was the smaller fish in front of the pack. It did not stay that way for long. The larger fish began gaining ground. The race was just getting under way, and so far, it seemed to be going well.

Almost **TOO** well.

The trail on which they were to follow seemed very smooth, but Finley knew that it would not stay that way.

He had overheard some of the older male fish talking about a section the contestants would have to swim through. According to them, it would be a dangerous spot.

Being filled with rough coral, you could easily tear your fins. If that were to happen, you were sure to lose the race, and if hurt bad enough, well...

Finley was not about to think about THAT possibility. He decided to concentrate on his form and speed.

Finley noticed that the larger fish seemed to be slowing down just a little. Because of their size, they tired a little faster than the smaller fish.

They were over halfway to the finish line!

Finley was actually out front and he noticed that the other fish who was just a bit larger than him was a close second.

All of a sudden, Finley saw the fish just behind him push past him so fast it was unbelievable!

THEN Finley saw the reason!

Mac had

SHOVED

the fish past Finley!

Mac was now **directly** beside Finley!

"I would rather lose to him than to a shrimp like you, but I don't intend to lose at all. It does not matter what I have to do to win. Do you understand, SHRIMP?" Mac sneered.

Finley did not reply. He kept his eyes on the path and his mind clear of fear.

Well, at least as clear as possible.

He was very scared, but he had made a promise to himself, and win or lose, he WOULD do his best!

They really did not have much farther to go.

THEN Finley saw the coral!

It was really thick and very jagged. He would have to be *careful* not to snag his fins. But...

That was not his only worry.

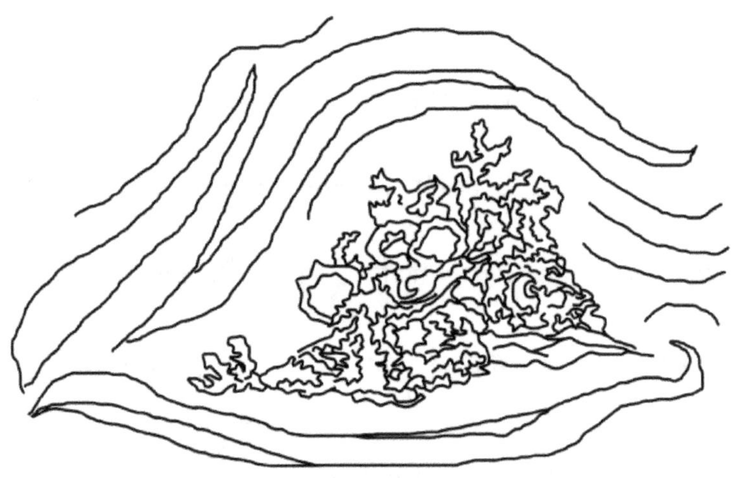

The current was swift and strong, and it took ALL of Finley's strength to stay on course.

To make matters worse, there were NO guards in this part of the race.

The guards were older fish with experience in this kind of water.

Finley thought it was *STRANGE* that they
would not be here in case of an emergency. He
did not have time to dwell on that right now
though.

Most of the fish had turned back because of
the conditions, and some of them just slowed
down to a pace where they would never be able
to catch up.

All that remained was...
      the fish Mac had pushed ahead...
        Mac himself...
          and of course, Finley.

With strength Finley did not know he had, he
pushed forward as hard as he could and swam
past the fish that was in lead. Leaving him and
Mac a decent length behind and being very close

to the finish line, Finley now felt he had a very good chance to win.

He was still not close enough to see the judge when he heard a HORRIBLE sound coming from behind. He knew if he slowed down to check it out he might lose the race.

The cries continued.

Finley knew someone was hurt. His conscience would not let him ignore the cries.

Just as Finley slowed down, Mac zoomed past him laughing.

"I told you, shrimp, NOTHING would stand in MY way of winning the prize."

Finley quickly turned back to see where the
cries came from.

He found the fish that had been in the lead
lying on the coral.

His fins were BADLY torn.

Finley assured the wounded fish he would
return quickly with help. Finley sped off toward
the finish line.

Mac was already receiving his prize. Finley
realized it did not really matter.

What DID matter was getting help.

He told the authorities about the wounded fish
on the coral.

Immediately, several fish went to rescue him!

They brought him to safety and called trained
fish to apply medicine to his torn fins.

They were all trying to comfort the hurt fish,
but he *would not* be quiet.

Finally, when they realized he needed to tell
them something, they grew quiet and listened.

"THAT FISH," he pointed to Mac, *"shoved me onto the coral on purpose!!!"*

The crowd became confused and angry. Everyone was yelling.

Someone in the crowd screamed, "He is trying to get away. Stop him!"

Two large fish caught Mac and held him securely as he struggled to get away.

The crowd was angry. They demanded the judge to take the prize away from him.

The situation became worse before he could make a decision.

A very large fish swam up to the judge and,
with a loud angry voice, declared that two
renegade fish had taken him hostage. He was
supposed to be a guard in the water near the
coral.

He believed it to be a plan so Mac could hurt
any fish in the lead so he could take the prize.

If the guard were out of the way, then there
would not be any witnesses.

Just as the guard finished speaking, some larger
fish swam out to the scene and found the two
fish who had taken the guard hostage.

They were part of the gang that attacked
Finley on the way to Grand Pappy's house!

Immediately, the fish in authority was called
over. When he arrived, he asked if anyone could
identify the troublemakers.

Challenger swam up and told all he knew about
them.

Mac and the two fish were taken away.

The judge declared Finley the

OFFICIAL WINNER

of the race because he was in the lead and
only lost because of turning back to help
someone.

Finally, it was all over. Finley and his family, and
his new friend were on their way to celebrate.

Grand Pappy Fin spoke first.

"I am SO proud of you.
You are a VERY brave fish."

"Thanks, Grand Pappy!" Finley said.

Challenger did what Challenger does best. He asked a question.

"How does it feel to be a winner?"

Finley smiled.

"It feels really good."

Finley *was* grateful that he won.

However...

He found out that winning is NOT the most important thing.

Doing the right thing is.

In his heart, he said a silent thank you to the Lord of the Heavens and the Earth and the Seas.

Finley now understood that faith and putting others first pleases Him. He felt certain there was more to discover about Him!

Until Then...

You Already Have Faith!

It's true! You already have faith. Finley had a desire to swim in a race. He wanted to win, but began to question whether or not he could because of his small size. At that time, he had more faith in failure than in winning. Thank goodness Grand Pappy Fin helped him change his thinking! When he realized that an ordinary man like Peter could walk on water as long as he looked at Jesus instead of himself or the storm, Finley knew that he must trust the Lord in all things. That way, no matter who won the race, he would always be a winner!

A Note from Finley

Hey there!

You know I was afraid to enter the race because I was smaller than most fish my age.

Actually though...

> I was afraid because I was scared I might FAIL.

I had to learn about faith, but you can't have faith in faith. You must have an object of your faith. That means you must trust in something or someone who has the ability to do the things that you can't.

In my case, I had to learn that the One who created me wants me to succeed and have a good life even more than I want it for myself!

He, The Lord, wants you to have a good life too! It does not mean that we won't have problems or disappointments. What it DOES mean is when we follow Him and His ways, we will make good choices. When things don't work out the way we wanted them to, He has a way of working them out for our good anyway.

What is it you want to do and haven't?

What is stopping you?

Maybe you think you are too small, too large, or too poor, or maybe you think you are not smart enough. Maybe you think you live in the wrong place or have the wrong family.

Many people won't try to do something they would like to do for many reasons but the truth is everything is about choice. You can choose to be mean or nice to others. You can choose to do the wrong things or choose to do the right thing. You can choose to stay where you are or go where you need to be to fulfill your dreams.

The greatest choice you will ever make is the choice to follow Christ.

Please remember following Christ is not about a bunch of rules. It is about developing a right relationship so you can know what He has for you.

The great thing is, you don't have to do it on your own!

He wants to be a part of your life!

These are some Scriptures that will help you, if you allow yourself to just believe.

1 Corinthians 1:27
2 Corinthians 12:9-10
Philippians 4:13

A Note from Challenger

Hi!

Do you always pick the right friends? Boy, I sure didn't!

For a long time, I swam with fish who always wanted to cause trouble and pick on other fish. I did things I was not proud of.

But there came a time in my life when I had to make a choice to change.

It is not easy to stand against the crowd, but I am glad I did. My life has been better because of taking a stand for what is right instead of doing what is popular.

Maybe you think you don't have a choice because of what you have done. But I learned some really good news!

God will never hold your past against
you if you truly repent and turn from
your wrong ways.

These Scriptures will help you start
making right choices.

2 Corinthians 5:17

Philippians 3:13

Galatians 6: 9-10

A Note from Jesus

Hello friend!

You've been learning about faith in this book. If you go to church, you have probably heard even more stories about Me.

Sometimes, these stories may seem to be impossible to believe. There are people who really don't know about Me, and then there are others who simply don't believe that I am real. Some may believe that I'm for real but they don't think they need Me today.

I lived on this earth a long time ago. I came here just like you. I was born as a baby with a mom and dad. I cried when I was hungry and I fell down and skinned my knees when I played.

In many ways I lived just like you!

The difference between me and you is that I really am God's son. I was there in Heaven when He created the world you live in. I helped hang the stars in the sky.

Seriously! I did!

Now, I know this is hard to understand because you might ask, "Where did you and God come from?"

Well, we are not the only ones that have always been. There is the Holy Spirit. He has always existed too. He helped Us create all things.

It might be hard for you to understand that We, (God the Father, God the Son, and God the Holy Spirit) have always existed. But that's where faith comes in. Just believe it.

Now you probably are wondering, "Are there three Gods?"

No, there is only one true God. We, (Father, Son and Holy Spirit) are three separate beings. We each do different things, but because we are all in total agreement and are totally perfect, we can be considered one. The only way to accept this without proof is to have faith that what I am telling you is true.

I cannot lie.

finley found out about faith. You can have it too!

You might be wondering, "If He was in Heaven doing cool stuff like hanging stars and creating angels and designing other planets (yes we did that too), why would He leave that and come to Earth as a baby?"

Well, I have to tell you I would have liked to stay with My father in Heaven. Everything there is perfect. There is no pain, no sickness, no sadness, no school, and no homework! Ha! In Heaven you can travel at the speed of thought! No kidding!

But My father needed a way to rescue the human race from the devil and all of his lies! He needed someone who had a perfect heart who would not sin and believe the devil and

all of his tricks that cause men to lie,
cheat, steal and kill.

He needed someone who was willing to come
with a clean heart and stay that way.

Why?

So that everyone on earth could see a
model of how to do it. That is why I came
as a baby so I could live among you to show
you the way. But that in itself was not
enough. There had to be someone with pure
blood, someone without sin that would be
willing to die for mankind so that all of you
might have a way to be in God's presence.

That being had to be me. Because I am His
Son, He needed me to come and die for you
to show you how much He loves you. I had
to totally trust Him. It took faith on my

part to know He had a perfect plan for all of us.

He is faithful and true!

He did not just allow me to die for you, but He also raised Me from the dead so you would know that you too could live again.

You might think that you are not so bad. Maybe you haven't done any real terrible things. In this book, Grand Pappy fin tells finley and Challenger a story about Me walking on the water. That actually happened! It was not just a made up story. I know you are probably wondering how that could really be true. Remember, I created the sea, so that gives me the right to walk on it!

This is what it boils down to.

I want to build a relationship with you!

It is not about going to church, although that is important for your spiritual growth. It is not even about what you can do or not do.

When you want to have a friendship with someone, you have to spend time with them. It is important to know what is important to them and for them to care what is important to you.

I want to spend time with you. Are you willing to spend time with Me?

You might ask, "How can I spend time with someone I can't see?"

Here is the answer. Talk to Me and Listen
for Me to talk to you. Read My Word,
the Bible. You will learn a lot about Me and
My ways. It will give you instructions on how
to live your life. It will give you direction
on how to have the best future. Trust me
to do what is best for you. You must
believe that Our Father in Heaven loves you.

Now, there is one more person you must
get to know. He is the Holy Spirit. Many
people get a little scared of Him because
they don't understand Him, but He is here
to look out for you. He also is with you to
help you know Me better. Read about Him
in the Book of John and Acts. You will see
Him in other books of the Bible but
especially in these two books. He is not
scary or spooky, but...

He is powerful!

When you are facing any kind of challenge, whether it's something like Finley's race or whether it's like Challenger's decision to change his choice of friends, the Holy Spirit will help you. In the Bible, He's actually called The Helper! He always leads you to know the Truth.

I will be waiting to hear from you!

Love,

Jesus

How to Read your Bible with Purpose

You may be a beginner at reading your Bible and have no idea of where or how to start. Perhaps you do read your Bible but you get frustrated when you don't understand what it means or how it applies to your real life.

You must remember this:
The Bible is communication between you and God.

His heart is not for you to become a Bible expert. It is to build a relationship with you.

These are some simple steps on how to read your Bible with purpose.

If you don't know where to start, read the New Testament first. The Gospel of John and Ephesians are good places to start.

1) Get a translation that you can understand.

2) Read a chapter a day. It takes about 15 minutes. If that is too much for you at the start, don't sweat it. It's not a race.

3) Ask yourself these questions.

   a. What jumps out at me? It might be a word, question or an overall idea.

   b. How will this change the way I live my life?

   c. What is my prayer for today? Don't forget that prayer is to communicate with God. Give Him a chance to speak back to you. He will! Remember to thank Him. He loves a grateful heart.

4) Keep a journal. Any kind of notebook will do. Write down what you get while reading and answer the questions above. Write your prayer down and you will be able to see when the answers come. Write down the date of your reading each day. You will enjoy going back to see your spiritual growth.

Do you Know Him?

If you have never accepted Jesus as Savior and Lord of your life, it is so simple. You should pray in your own words and remember He is not grading you on how right or well you pray. He looks at your heart, but it is good to say it out loud. This will sound a little strange to you at first but do it anyway! Your prayer can go something like this:

Dear Father God,

I know that you sent Your Son Jesus Christ to die on the cross a long time ago to pay for all my sins. I receive Your forgiveness by faith. I know I can do nothing to be good enough but because of Your grace and mercy, You accept me and You will change my heart. You did it for me so we could have a relationship because you loved me so much. I can now have eternal life and have a full life on this earth. Thank you for hearing and accepting my repentance. Teach me how to live a life pleasing to you.

Amen

If you prayed this prayer and believed in your heart, you are now a brand new person. All the old things have gone and all things are new. Let the Lord change you. All you have to do is learn how much He loves you.

Here are some Scriptures to help you understand salvation.

- o John 3:16-17
- o 2 Corinthians 5:17-21
- o Ephesians 2:8-10

Read the first chapter of Ephesians and know that all of those promises are for you!

I would love to hear from you if this book has impacted your life. God Bless You.

My web address is www.sandystarnes.com.

About the Author

Sandy Starnes has a heart to show children of all ages how much God loves them. She enjoys teaching others how to live a life pleasing to Him. She has four grandchildren and lives in York, SC.

About the Illustrator

Holly Payne wants others to know that God is loving, faithful and lots of fun. She enjoys bringing words to life through drawing, writing, publishing books like the Finley books and speaking.

Read Them All!

Book # 1 (Blue Cover)

Finley the Fish with Tales from the Sea of Galilee:

A Story of Faith

Book # 2 (Green Cover)

Finley the Fish with Tales from the Sea of Galilee:

A Story of Purpose